I Won't Be/long Here

I Won't Be/long Here

Poems by

Lisa Masé

Cover design by Shay Culligan

ISBN: 978-1-954353-27-5

Kelsay Books
502 South 1040 East, A-119
American Fork, Utah, 84003

Acknowledgments

Many thanks to the publications in which versions of the following poems have appeared, occasionally with different titles:

Angles Journal: "All-American Cake"
Heron Clan Review: "Papi Mi Ha Insegnato"
Infinite Rust: "Jetlag"
Inlandia Journal: "Rose Hope"
Jacar Press One: "What's Worth Keeping"
Long Island Review: "Origins"
Prime Number Magazine: "Chihuly over Venice"
Pudding Magazine: "Petrarca of the Euganei"
Red Coyote Press: "Senior Year"
Silver Needle Press: "Bread Ghazal"
Switchgrass Review: "Migraine"
Toe Good Poetry: "Raised in Mother Mary's Image"
Unearthed Magazine: "Letter to My Mom," "How I Am American"

Contents

Letter to My Mom

My eyes welled when you wouldn't leave your bed
for three days at a time with no explanation except a migraine.

Your suffering bounced off the cold marble floors
of our apartment.

I wanted to avenge you, but there were too many culprits:

your father sitting on the porch with a shotgun
when you missed curfew;
your mother running away with the car salesman
to buy another pair of red pumps;
your church demanding a dollar every Sunday
when your allowance was only 50 cents.

After four miscarriages you were born, blue and silent
until the nurse gave you oxygen behind privacy drapes
at the Kansas City Children's Hospital in 1941.

Raising your babies in Italy kept you from getting burned
until you had to return to Kansas,
walk over the coals of your memories,
care for the failing parents who could not care for you.

You don't believe you're crazy, but crazy has been rising slowly
inside you since before you were born, a candle left to singe
your mother's dining room curtains
after all the voices in your head had stumbled to bed.

You aren't able to dampen the flames that generations of women
have fanned into the blaze I see behind those narrowing eyes.
You rub throbbing temples and let the fire
of your Welsh-turned-Midwest heritage burn you down.

I am making a reduction of my life so I might understand yours.

Bread Ghazal

My father taught me that fenugreek, caraway,
and fennel are the secrets to our rye bread.

Hard enough to crack under a fist,
we call it by its German name: *schuettelbrot.*

Every fall, we stocked Nonna's cellar
with newspaper-wrapped stacks of this hard tack bread.

After moving to the States, I spent a year researching
the Roma, who carried spices in their caravans for bread.

They brought fenugreek, caraway, and fennel
from North Asia, wouldn't let those seeds drop
until they reached a safe place to bake their *moro.*

The Alps became this haven, and rye sourdough
has been handed down ever since, bubbling
into the staple with which we were bred.

When I go home to Italy, grains are not the villains
they have become for America's
health-obsessed disdainers of bread.

Instead, they are revered as keepers
at the chapel door of seasons: there is strength
to persevere if one at least has bread.

Fenugreek cleanses the fluid body,
caraway disinfects, and fennel helps digest
what may be too dense about Lisa's *pane.*

Origins

Brother, you slide an *Amarone* bottled in 1992
from your Vermont farm house wine rack
where it dutifully collects telling dust.
It's ten years old and could age another ten.

No one ever told us we would move across the Atlantic
and end up in the same state.

"Dalla cantina di Nonna Dina": You name our grandmother's
cellar, cool even in summer's noon.

I remember being sent down there to fetch something,
how dread and delight seized me as I imagined
what might lurk behind that oak door:

mold-mottled sausages dangling from top shelves
where Fontina wheels would peer with butter-dulled rinds;

shiny jars of apricot jam, proud brown bottles of elderberry syrup,
dried wild mushrooms bagged in muslin and crusty rye bread
wrapped in newspaper—
all preserved with the patience of mountains.

There, gleaming with egg wash on the marble work table,
I would spot my charge: *crostata di mele.*
Bravely I carried the apple tart upstairs.

When you show me this wine in your kitchen,
I remember the flavor of apples picked that morning,
the melt of spring butter over latticed crust,
and a grandmother who splashed wine into our water
to make us stronger.

Papi Mi Ha Insegnato

"Luzellette mi ha insegnato," **Papi** would explain
how she had taught him to dig under fallen oak leaves
for morels after spring rain, to scour southern slopes
for boletes and chantrelles once summer solstice waned,
to respect the fierce red amanitas and let them go by.

Papi and I decide to make egg-basted asparagus,
a recipe from great grandmother Luzellette,
Little Bird, who lived and died in Gaby
near an Alpine stream that bouldered down
the steep slopes she walked with pack basket
and sickle to harvest fresh grass for her goats.

Nothing but goat milk, potatoes, and polenta
in those war years. He leaned not to get kicked
while milking, to hide milk in the stone house
where it waited for hungry neighbors
who had sold their animals for flour.

We cook the asparagus recipe so it will not
be forgotten, told every time it is prepared
to honor the first truth of green spears
finding their way through black dirt, earth arrows
that we gather and steam before they grow
delicate fronds that make seeds like tiny globes.

Easter Picture

On our way to church, Mom in her coral jacket
(that I would inherit in high school)
holds our hands in front of a forsythia, first spring gold.

My father the photographer calls for a smile, counts off,
and Guido, proud in his navy suit, decides to grin
through his freckles instead of making his usual fish face.

I am the one who has something to say
in my pink-rimmed glasses and yellow dress with white lace.
The snapshot captures me, arms flung skyward,
head tilted back, leaving the others behind.

Raised in Mother Mary's Image

The nuns would check for a handkerchief
tucked into my uniform pocket, token needed
to enter the marbled archways of Sant'Orsola School.

Riding to school on the bar of my brother's bicycle,
I rocked side to side and laughed like crazy:
it seemed impossible that we could fall.

Lessons always ended with church: waiting my turn
to swing the frankincense censer, I would
bite off my pinky nail and curse.

Too short to reach our apartment's gold doorbell,
I propped the oak door open with a brick
when I was sent for milk before dinner.

By evening, my ponytail ached until Mom took it out
and I could curl up in bed, read my lessons, dream of anthills
and Etruscans with *La Vergine* always watching.

Summers on the Adriatic

Forever your little sister, growing up
on the shoals of love you would not give,
unnoticed despite your agonizing scrutiny,
swimming in the eddies of daydreams,

I was stunned each time your bicycle tire
bumped mine and made me swerve, hit pavement,
watch blood rise from scabbed knees
as a breeze brought the faint fragrance
of honeysuckle and sea brine.

My Brother

Coyotes anchor the full moon
from the other side of the mountain.
My mood anxious, yours confident,
we seek the protection of Nonna Dina's house,

seated one step away from dark forest.
You are sure as the sweetest jam in her cellar
that the fox walking we learned
to keep silent would save us once again.

You close the door slowly, its inevitable click
amplified by the yearning to not be heard.
We slip under comforters, still wearing
our jackets, as the moon rises above tree line.

What would our parents understand
the next morning from the state of our hair,
from pants pockets lined with pine needles
as we cram our hands inside them, act casual?

Guide to Ferrara

Medieval city ruled by the Estense family
until Renaissance fizzled, Ferrara
may have been forgotten, but
it comes alive after dark in the *Torrione,*
erected as a watchtower against
Turkish invasion at the mouth
of *Corso Porta Mare,* road
that leads to the ocean.

The Bora wind chills from Yugoslavia
as we race up the staircase to get inside
this twenty-sided tower
built with hand-made bricks.

"Per fortuna," Papi sighs,
"Ottomans did not invade."
Stereo blasts Tower of Power,
bartender sips a glass of red
with five men at the bar,
some polished in silk and gold chains,
others bedraggled in Adidas and berets.
A soul quintet blows Horace Silver,
echoes against the round walls
of a bastion turned swing joint.

We walk home along the *Mura,*
fortress walls whose ruddy structure
still holds true, towered by oak
and linden that bend to protect us
from midnight drizzle.

Sabbiona Cloister

We leave Ferrara after dark,
headed for our ancestral Dolomites,
blind to changing landscape
until the moon emerges and reveals
that we traded the Po River plains
for steep peaks protected
by Holy Ones.

I roll down the window,
hear cloister songs echo
from a rocky fortress
high above the autostrada
built with the same stone
that harbors sisters praying.

Everyone knows
they devote their lives
to spirit, yet no one
is allowed inside
to touch the secret,

that which was never born
but lives in the mountain,
blessed by the bright moon
and the moonless night.

November First in Italy

Mother Mary's sanctuary with walls built from river stones
marks the southern corner of a garden too old for an owner.
Its single steeple bell has been ringing every hour since dawn.

I turn over, eyes closed, pull the comforter closer,
let my warm body rest one more moment as snow
cloaks craggy peaks at sunrise on All Saints' Day.

Memories of hikes for flower bouquets and wild mushrooms,
nights spent shaping marzipan under lamp light too dim:
I must walk to keep them alive.

I wrap myself in shawls, join the procession
carrying a wooden Mary dressed in chipping paint and gold leaf
from the downtown cathedral to her winter chapel.

She will watch over gardens and graves all winter.

Zia Rita stays home as her mother would have,
whips eggs into cake batter, dips chestnuts in chocolate,
simmers soup beans, chops vegetables in offering.

Petrarca of the Euganei

As poet, he kept ten ink wells,
wrote to please persimmons
so they might ripen
before the bear of winter
took them to her den.

As priest, he gleaned pomegranates
before Hades could count
on too many grey months,
hardened his sermons when fire
would not warm the hearths
of shivering villagers.

As public official, he collected
leather-bagged *lira* from farmers
who herded goats and cows
along the Appenine mountain spine.

He would have preferred
to trade cheese for their servitude,
return to his home of river stone walls
and wine-bottle windows,
light a taper and eat pecorino
with grapes and bread.

Chihuly over Venice

Loredana Balboni had heard the tromping
of paint-splattered shoes across her balcony,
even glimpsed the eye-patched man more
than once, but never thought to mention him
to her sister Letizia or suggest they invite
him to sip Prosecco from crystal flutes
that, while dazzling under a glass chandelier
at one of their seasonal *feste,* paled against
the green grandeur of the glass this gap-toothed man
blew in his Pilchuck workshop overlooking the quiet water
of Puget Sound, so unlike the rising canals of Venice
it's a wonder he ever found his way to *La Biennale.*

Or maybe she sent him away so she could
marvel at the sculpture entirely alone, lie
beneath it on her balcony by candle light,
wake up and take her gondola into Canal Grande,
point to it with a grimace, pretending she had no
idea how it had landed, suspended above
her palazzo as though opera singers
had wailed out each tail-tipped sphere
during a midnight performance of *La Traviata*
at *Gran Teatro La Fenice,* voices rising from ashes
as glass does, singing itself to life from a million
grains of sand hiding inside each line
that the sculptor breathed out of fire.

Testamento

C'era una volta una donna—
Once upon a time there was a woman
who knew that words shaped the world
round as her womb, round as the cycle
of seasons that brought wheat for bread.

Ti ricordi? Do you remember
that you are this mother, sister, lover?
Does your blood touch earth with every
returning moon, feed soil that feeds food?

C'era una volta un tempo senza tempo—
Once upon a time there was no time.
Full moon shone over dark soil
so rivers could travel past boulders
and diamonds to meet oceans.

*Non é mai finito—*it is never done,
because blood rises with the tides
each new moon then returns the womb
to the earth that created her.

What's Worth Keeping

If no one had told you your grandmother
was unstable, refused her lithium
and kept a kitchen drawer stuffed
with packages of cream-filled chocolate
cupcakes, you might have looked back
on that American chapter with the fondness
some have for their memories.

You could never have imagined
that Wednesday afternoons with Papi
shaping dough into pumpkin ravioli
and braising foraged mushrooms
in your apartment kitchen would end
so you could know second grade in Kansas.

What if it didn't matter that your parents
left Italy to spend a year drilling for fresh water
in Somalia, took you from cobblestoned
Ferrara to live with Midwest grandparents?

What would remain of those days
eating boiled hot dogs with pickle relish
on white buns, going barefoot into
the backyard, crouching down for mint,
eating it but not daring to share it with friends
who would never come over anyway?

When you returned to Italy, it was not you
who emerged but a stunned girl wearing
the delicate gold bracelet her father gave her
(as though it would make up for it all),
a third grader who stayed after school
until she'd memorized her times tables.

The Songs Become My Home

I sing an immigrant song of two homes,
raised in a medieval city studded with cobblestones
where divination with *tarocchi* was born
between incantations chanted in candle light,

taken to a cow town that croons in middle America,
a suburb consumed by pavement drawing lines
between ranches and mansions where country club gates
are open only when the price is right.

I sing a simple song so I will not forget how pasta needs
the freshest eggs and bread is made from mother dough
with grain milled tender between smooth stones
in a land of olive trees that reach to the sky for centuries.

Jetlag

Biting wind tugs at the sails
of morning. I squeeze my eyes shut
as if they could keep out
the rude American sunrise.

How could it be
that an almost sleepless night
has already hooked me
into tomorrow, floundering
for a single dream whose whisper
ebbs on the shores of my mind?

Sweating, I flash on the lights
at midnight to see myself alone
without the land that birthed me
in Montebelluna, Mountain
of the Beautiful Moon, raised me

italiana in an ironed school uniform,
patient for summer days spent
making *marmellata* with Nonna Dina
and soaking in rosemary sun.

Sun rises but I wish it were night,
standing on dream shores where
longing twists peaks and branches
floating on waning light.

When We Moved to the States

I know now that it was necessary to leave Papi,
help Mom usher aging parents to the other side.
Party dresses, rock collection and my red record player
had to stay behind. "You'll outgrow it all anyhow."

We made our way to the Missouri River, steamboat channel
swallowed me whole, spat me out muddy with teenage slang
that my British tutors could never have taught me.

I went to the Rhumba Box for indie punk shows
before it closed down. The cops said it was a fire hazard
but I never believed them, kept squatting there anyway
and smoking weed on the roof with Sarah Present.

Eventually they caught me dosing Robitussin in Loose Park
after sunset. The next morning, DARE officers showed up
at our house, lectured me about PCP and Angel Dust
while my mom sat stunned on the piano bench in her red bathrobe.

Late-Night Grilled Cheese

You will need:
2 slices white bread, preferably Wonder
2 tablespoons (or more) salted butter
3 American cheese slices in plastic wrappers, unwrapped

Method:
Spread butter on each slice of bread.

Heat a skillet on the stove. Turn it down to medium low heat
and place one slice of bread on it, butter side down.

Hear it sizzle.

Place cheese slices on top of the sizzling bread.

Then, place the second slice of bread on top of the cheese,
butter side up.

Cook on low heat for a couple of minutes.
While you wait, roll a joint and tuck it behind your ear for later.

Flip the sandwich with a wide spatula. Press it down gently.
Listen to the butter melting. Breathe in the aroma
of spring cow pastures as you remember them, even though
the cows whose milk made this butter never tasted grass.

Rip off a sheet of aluminum foil and lay it flat on the counter.

Check the bottom of the sandwich. When it is crisped
to your liking, scoop out the sandwich and place it on the foil.
Wrap it up and take it to the Rhumba Box.

Tomorrow, Mom will chide you for leaving the skillet on the stove.
Try to remember to turn off the burner.

Senior Year

The difference between wrong and right
is crumbling, rubble in the tracks of dusty promises
that cold November rain can't wash away.

We drive away in your Astro van, me crying
for everything I know will come after,
the dissonance between wrong and right.

"Why are you crying?" You ask on the highway.
I light a cigarette, let smoke wrap the pain
that cold November rain can't wash away.

I can't explain the grey days that transpired
when you spent last summer with her, muddling
the distinction between wrong and right.

Pulling up to Chubby's Diner as the radio
wails Counting Crows, you stop to dry the tears
that cold November rain can't wash away.

We sit silently in the parking lot, holding
hands as our four years together fill
the distance between wrong and right
that cold November rain can't wash away.

How I Am American

I sit with a tape recorder and my ninth grade spiral notebook
listening to Grammy Ruth weave memories so thick
my pencil will not move across the page anymore from the weight

of great grandmother Elizabeth's horseback journey
across Three Forks of the Wolf River in Kentucky
to chase her husband, brick mason for wild west towns.

They sold the table and chairs that came on the ship
from Wales and bought a covered wagon with four draft horses
that would deliver them all the way to Kansas City.

She could not have known that soon after their baby was born,
her husband would die of typhoid while mortaring outposts
for Westport, gateway to the Santa Fe Trail.

The recorder stops like a gunshot but her story takes flight
from the Great Plains of sorrow where a woman
raised her daughter alone and lands on a stone
at the Wolf River's shore, minstrels the tale that time forgot.

Migraine

Nothing like her
but it's inescapable:
she made me, running
from her manic mother
who owned too many pairs
of red shoes for her size five feet.

Memories would turn
into monthly migraines, keep
her in bed with the shades drawn
while I asked her to comb
my hair, boil me an egg, read
my poems, to no avail.

I spent six years with those
size five shoes because
my mother needed me
to keep her from going dark
like my grandmother finally
would, loony as they come,
making me cram my size nine
feet into her shiny pumps.

Now I am mother
turning back in wonder
at my daughter running barefoot
down the pebbled path in the rain,
looking for worms.

Rose Hope

When she could not have a garden,
Mom grew fourth story balcony
geraniums. Wrought-iron railing
framed flood plains beyond
the medieval Italian town
where ocean rose at the end
of the cypress-lined road.

She scanned the horizon
for Kansas, a constant place
where roses would grow.

The Plains returned to her
when long-distance phone calls
could not replace the only child.
Forced to return, she cared for
the parents who had driven her away.

Back in the States, she raises roses
like children now, cups thin-veined
blossoms between small hands, never
lets one wilt on a thorny branch,
keeps them vased in the kitchen.
Their spectral fragrance
lets her forget that, once, she escaped.

Allergic Reaction

You were always lacquering your nails
with hot pink polish after acetone
removed chipped layers, shards
picked off from your fidgeting
that trailed through our apartment.

As soon as you unscrewed the bottle top
of neon America I closed my bedroom door,
retreated from that smell, chose
Alice in Wonderland from the bookshelf.

The first time I tried nail polish at age four,
my heart stopped. I withered to the bathroom floor.
You rushed me to the hospital. Breath returned.

My Father Gave Me Art

Nonna Dina believed geology would be more practical:
Papi got his degree and studied art in night school.
His oil portraits of composers and strangers
watched over our dining room as we savored
the pumpkin tortellini he made from scratch on Wednesdays.

I memorized the way his pinky rolled hand-cut squares
of pasta dough into ravioli, how his thumb bent backwards
just like mine as he printed fork marks into gnocchi.

Now his knuckles curl around arthritis.
Still he picks up the paintbrush to show my toddler
how hands are channels of grief and praise in grey and blue.
"Lei ha il dono." She has the gift, he proclaims
as her bold strokes decipher the sky in watercolor.

Why You Stayed Behind

Budding girl who chose shoulder cuts at the butcher's
with you, Papi, so we could make roast together,
daughter of vegetable markets and pasta shops,
letting my skin soak it in like the slanted light
that raced with us as we pedaled home,

I came up with you as my center, gleaning
every slice of wisdom you imparted, from recipes
repeated because they were never written
to geology lessons about every stone in my collection.

Before I moved to Kansas City with Mom,
I begged you to let me stay in our apartment
with marble floors cool even in summer's swelter,
to let me attend high school with my friends,
to keep riding my pink bike for *gelato*
at the *caffè* that would tune into Top 40 radio.

I thought you were exiling me from our orbit
because my risotto wasn't perfect.

In the Midwest, kids rode their bikes without destination.

The markets were odorless: plastic-wrapped super stores.

You came to visit for Christmas and Easter.
I ran away to the drug-addled land of assimilation.

All-American Cake

For the cake:
3 cups white flour
2 cups white sugar
1 cup butter
3 egg whites, beaten
1 teaspoon Oaxacan vanilla extract
1/2 teaspoon Sri Lankan cinnamon
A pinch of Passamaquoddy sea salt

For the icing:
1 cup butter
1 cup white sugar
1 teaspoon Oaxacan vanilla extract
1 1/2 ounces Colombian single source dark chocolate (70% dark chocolate or more)

If you have access to an oven, preheat it to 350 degrees.

Cream together the butter and sugar. Use white sugar
from a mill operated by the people of Barbados because
there is no longer a market their traditional molasses,
raw sugar cane boiled down into mineral-rich syrup.

Find butter from grass-fed cows raised by migrant laborers
who produce most of the dairy products in the Northeast
to support their families in Vera Cruz.

Gently fold in the flour. Try to find flour milled from heirloom
European wheat whose strain is still pure.

Sprinkle in the Sri Lankan cinnamon powdered from the bark
of this Laurel family tree, used sparingly in tea and savory dishes
from Morocco to China until the Portuguese took over its trade.

Add the Oaxacan vanilla. Lace the cake with this rare
orchid that only grows wild in Chinantla forests where farmers
pollinate in the morning, await the harvest of long, black beans
with tiny seeds that they heat and dry to make vanilla extract.

You might forget the Passamaquoddy sea salt,
because the people who harvest it where chased from their land
in 1607 and returned after British settlers had renamed it Maine.
Don't forget the salt, or your cake will be tasteless.

Separate the egg yolks from the whites.
Beat the egg whites until they form peaks stiff as soldiers.

Grease two cake tins with butter and divide the batter
between them, separating them to prevent insurgence
from the vanilla and cinnamon.

Bake at 350 degrees for 35 minutes, or until a toothpick inserted
comes out clean.

While the cake is baking, remember your own cake tradition.

My Italian grandmother made a cake with Alpine buckwheat flour
and apricot jam simmered from fallen fruit we would find
in the grove nearby. She sweetened it with the local honey
and added eggs from chickens scratching in the farmer's yard.

As the cake cools, make the icing.
Over a double boiler, cream together the butter and sugar.
Add the vanilla slowly, watching the mixture turn darker.
Let the chocolate melt with the other ingredients in a double boiler.

You will never know if it's from Caquetá or Cordoba because the label doesn't reveal the work of farmers who harvest it, clean beans from their placenta, ferment, roast, and grind them. This chocolate icing recipe makes a double batch.

When sharing this recipe, please include all of it.

About the Author

Lisa Masé (she/they) writes about family, food, geography, and the invisible thread that weaves them. She is a translator, holistic nutritionist, food sovereignty activist, parent, and land steward from Italy, now living on occupied Abenaki land in Vermont.

www.ingramcontent.com/pod-product-compliance
Lightning Source LLC
Chambersburg PA
CBHW031154090426
42738CB00008B/1334